owlmouth

New Women's Voices Series, 150

poems by

Michele Marie Desmarais

Finishing Line Press
Georgetown, Kentucky

owlmouth

New Women's Voices Series, 150

ACKNOWLEDGMENTS

Marsi (thank you) to the editors of publications in the U.S. and Canada in
which some of these poems first appeared:

American Indian Culture And Research Journal: "owlmouth," "this winter is
an owl," "sweetgrass."
Descant: "egress."
Full—An Anthology of Moon Poems: "egress."
Interdisciplinary Studies in Literature and the Environment (ISLE): "a
traveling song."
The Malahat Review—Indigenous Perspectives Issue: "the aviary."
Room—Canada's Oldest Literary Journal By and About Women: "setting, the
table," "taking leave," (36.1 Mythologies of Loss); "change," "translating 'owl,'"
(38.1 In Translation).
*Yellow Medicine Review—A Journal of Indigenous Literature, Art and
Thought*: "a troublesome relationship with owls."

A film of "sweetgrass" is on permanent display at the University of Nebraska
State Museum's *First Peoples of the Plains: Traditions Shaped By Land & Sky*
exhibit.

Publisher: Leah Maines
Editor: Christen Kincaid
Cover Art: Cami Cavanaugh Rawlings
Author Photo: Cami Cavanaugh Rawlings
Cover Design: Elizabeth Maines McCleavy

Printed in the USA on acid-free paper.
Order online: www.finishinglinepress.com
also available on amazon.com

Author inquiries and mail orders:
Finishing Line Press
P. O. Box 1626
Georgetown, Kentucky 40324
U. S. A.

Table of Contents

For
Judy Boss
Ben Nauslar
& my Dad
with love
& gratitude
for the good tracks
home

owlmouth

owlmouth is silence
small bones buried
away from ceremony

death dropped a feather
call it knowledge, call it school
or english, words curved
hard into beak

into the language of treaty
of quantum, blood meant
for owls, death eyes deciding
the lives of our time

they taught us to speak
words that contain the wing shadow of owls
they wanted us to learn
one hundred words for genocide

what didn't they say
which is why we speak now
kiss the owl in our minds
goodbye

taanshi
taanshi kiya
nimiyo-ayaan
marsi

a traveling song

where the old ones sang
water wandered
away
out of words

all august the sky
in a coal dress
refused
to dance

in the skin of land
stories burn, become
new scars
why animals run

tell me what ceremonies
we need
now
this bird
lies in my hands
with eyes
like strange stones
that do not see

a troublesome relationship with owls

blame them
blame the owls
piss-whiskey eyes
startle from shadow
from trees where light
fell
asleep

no name called
but trace the cause:
everything happened last year
in claws that tore
bark from bone

grief shapes a tree
a rabbit
a mouse
anyone
my friend
for this
we all die
in the stories
of owls

and here
we are
again

owls
there might be
ceremonies
but in this mean
time
i hold a shot
glass
before the face
see
through this my eyes
turn
a similar
hue
we must be
related

owls
death in a lit house
looks back
at you
so here's a toast:

to what remains
what will remain
who

setting, the table

you go into this book
and become a bear
words form a muzzle
ink blackens your eyes
while rhythm patters
its way down a trail
line after line
it secretly
gathers your thoughts
into smell: rain
berries bleeding
their scent onto
wind
fir trees cradling
a history of
storm

you were just reading a book
now you are bear
and distant as sleep or thunder
you nod,
you can hear me
you nod,
you will bite
our sophistical table
is where you gnaw
bones till they crack
grief across my tongue
we share more than most
observe
the setting becomes
a habitual wonder
there are ursine endings
to each meal
to every book

gazes averted we possess
the propriety of animals
but even so
i will not tear myself back
from knife and fork
from civil rage
nor you from these chronic
mutinies of fur
more credible, apparently
than my cutlery or marriage

canoe

he always needed her
like the time she came home
two hours late
and found him huddled
drunk
out back in the alley
a small deeper blackness
crouched among garbage and glass
his face bloodless
against her hands
she traced
the carved lines
of concrete wall
down his cheek
navigating despair

i need you he said
his breath cold on her neck
we're in this together

taking leave

this night the sea
is drunk
just like
any one
she drops
her head
low
snuggles
on the shoulder
of a land
any land
and calls those next
hours home

then
she leaves
weaves away
the way a girl
shoes in hand
slides out
of a room
into dawn
headache pink
and heaving
heaving
with birdsong

by this ocean
by now
you should know
i don't know
much else
but this ocean
you should know
right now
her waves
and this drunken
leave
taking
leave

our lady of the owls

i went the way
they said
no child should go
call it
the edge of the forest
or school
i became
what they expected
one with a life
foreign even to me
our lady of the owls
a winter count of loss

frozen vision:
girl
holding up the lamppost
holding up a sky
silver pumps
blue fishnet stockings
not even shivering

the city almost cures memory

she wonders
is it still a homecoming
if everyone
is dead

or if all they do
remember
is the beauty
as she left

liminal

now i am
thin
as a
stick

i need you
to throw me
further
away

this is
meant
for fire

a limb
where owls
dream

the aviary

she began when birds
fell from her mouth
instead of words

sometimes sparrow
sometimes hawk
often mourning

doves grey and sad
with stories perched
scratched the kitchen table

impossible alphabets
scarred her home
there were no songs

she drank
her prayers
turned into owls

death dropped feathers
she bathed in dust
floored

until one raven
hungry
pecked at a pen

then simple
as sound or sky
everything began
to change

like weather for wings

egress

first toes lengthen, yellow
talons emerge curve like stories
he is horrified
ugly, he says, *ugly*
try a pedicure or something
jesus christ
i shut the door
crouch on the edge
of a bathroom sink
claws clench curl loosen
to the red bang of blood

next week is the thinning
i have blue in the bones
an addiction to sky
grows like a nest in mind
i want wind to have its way
why these walls?
with widening eyes
i watch small corner movements
memory becomes a shadow hop
the moon reminds me
constantly of rabbit
through the mad shaping of mouth
i know i can sing
besieged by words
demanding reply
a mighty yelp hurtles me
finally
to the greening peace of cedar
and all this insistent light

the door
the locks
are awkward but

i am going
out.

a report from the birds

the city
i was dreaming
had no birds
the sky was
feather absent
without song

there were
shadows
on glass
shaped like
shattered angels
a final
report
from the birds

we leave you
searching
for direction

i hold
those words now
in my hands
like strange stones
we will not see

this winter is an owl

pretend this winter is an owl
once in a lifetime storms
common now as feathers, grey
unsuitable for light

a tree remembers long claws
years beneath dreams or death
but nothing like this, everything
turning owl in sickness

the car has a wing
oil fields feather their nests
lawns, chemical drunk
yellow like jaundiced eyes
we know

a flock of owls
is not a murder
but a parliament
talk about irony
just don't pretend this winter
isn't an owl
their inaction, my despair
your next trip to the mall

the tipping point

everywhere they weren't
owls dance
their talons
scar
straight lines
like pipes
across the land

the tripping point

on the plains
iktomi walks
wears eight
rubber boots
says *the rivers*
are tricky
these days
guess it's an uprising

sweetgrass—a poem in three parts

i.

iktomi is walking
one
by
one
by
one
by
one
by
one
by
one
by
one
he
taps
a
word
up
each
stem
a
long
green
story

ii.

go north after custer
move
from untaken skies

to school
in one generation
the kids return
if lucky return
wrung thin
mute with christ
when you're drinking up heaven
it's hard to find medicine
so we disappear
again almost ghosts
but stubborn
right as stone
away from schools
to a homeless coast
where we live
raise up children
with memories that smell
like cedar smoke
returning one day
to our plains
i carry a good
story of salmon
for the earth
who laughs
says *i've seen the ocean*
says *that hair down your back*
reminds me of family
of time
and all you relatives
long
long
like a braid
of sweet
sweet
grass

iii.

light is a secret
we speak in dark tongues
as we curl together
tangleturntwist
till something says
up
the world says
up
and green the i extends
suddenly
to blue so far
to rise up more
while bursting with roots
with joy to spark thunder
to call all beings
here
all good beings
here
and even iktomi
who's coming here
now
with a story
for us
that is
about
eight
feet
tall

translating 'owl'

ulūka
my sanskrit owl
vāhana, vehicle of lakṣmī
sharing the name with
a muni, sage
that term from silence
itself
ulūka
a kind of grass
sound in grass
perhaps
ulūka
the quiver i feel
crossing cultures
deva-nāgarī
the script
a divine city
the arrival of language

aen yiiboo
hiåhaå
michif
dakota
owl
english
dread as i pass
mixed
translating blood
liminal as feather

ulūka
aen yiiboo
hiåhaå
owl

words don't become you
translate this, for instance:

the absent sound
as you dive
from branch to life
the breath
beneath you
as it leaves
limned with silence

it's as simple as sound or sky

no
harm
no
owl

change (medicine)

they might have noticed
the bear
whose movement
down the sidewalk
resembled a private waltz
or hard-won swagger
that comes from knowing
trails, from soft leaf language
from the tricky custom of rivers
all this
they might have seen
coming down that street

where thought-bones
became walls
piled so high
the bit of blue
might be sky
might be buffalo
might be buffalo china
might be blue jeans
where they instructed:
measure out mystery
construct
by creating more bones
chew till your teeth crack
or someone brings medicine

this is how things change

skins conceal
but not entirely
dreams edge out
in four directions
like paws
with quiet purpose
coming closer

take time to notice
there are good tracks
now
down these streets
the air smells of
cedar, sage
tobacco and sweetgrass
with minds made fit
for green and life
we begin again
our words grow bright wings
take flight in possible skies
our thoughts gather in
their bones, their fur
their grace and remember
to walk
with gratitude

this is how things change

years from now
someone will
most certainly stop
at that corner
and say
i heard this story
about a bear

home

here there are ravens
who speak a language
so old there are no words
for wall, fence or human
silvered with rain
the ravens translate
from stone to salal
to fur, tree
and ocean

come home
when you can
and know
they still know you
despite your modern tongue
lit with quick time
the tricky
skins you wear
in that city
the owl who
death dances
through your mind

come home
when you can
scrape history bare
return to where
a raven
will rattle
your story
back to brightness
until it shines
like a star
fringed with night
cedar
salt-scented wind

come home
come home
where every path
can speak
where each tree
is long as a dream
come home
come home
let the ravens
remind you
that we are an old song
together
stone, salal
fur, tree
feather and ocean
and ocean

come home
when you can
one day
a day
perhaps the ravens
already remember
and they will tell you
again
that you are
home
that you are
from this place
this very place
where even
the humans
are poets

D r. Michele Marie Desmarais is a Canadian poet and scholar of Métis, Dakota and European descent. She was raised and educated in Vancouver, British Columbia on the unceded traditional territories of the Coast Salish peoples of the Musqueam, Squamish, and Tsleil-Waututh Nations. Michele is an Associate Professor in Religious Studies and a teaching faculty member in the Native American Studies program at the University of Nebraska at Omaha (UNO), where she was also the founding director of Medical Humanities. Her book, *Changing Minds: Mind Consciousness and Identity in Patañjali's Yoga-sūtra and Cognitive Neursocience* (Motilal Banarsidass), was selected as one of the foundational texts in the field of science and religion by the International Society for Science and Religion.

Michele's poetry has been published widely in literary journals, including: *American Indian Culture and Research Journal; International Studies in Literature and the Environment; Yellow Medicine Review; Room Magazine; Contemporary Verse2; Descant;* and *The Malahat Review.* A film of her reciting her poem "Sweetgrass" is part of the University of Nebraska State Museum's First Peoples of the Plains exhibit and her poetry is included in the Native American Artists Resource Collection of the Heard Museum (Phoenix, Arizona). Michele is a grateful past recipient of a Canada Council for the Arts Aboriginal Writer's grant. She currently performs and records with her band, owlmouth.

Michele has a BA in Psychology from Simon Fraser University, an MA in Religious Studies from the University of British Columbia, and a PhD in Asian Studies also from U.B.C. Michele's areas of specialty include: medical humanities; Indigenous fine arts and pedagogy; mindfulness; spirituality and wellness; Sanskritic thought; mad studies; Yoga psychology; and religion and film.